Show Day

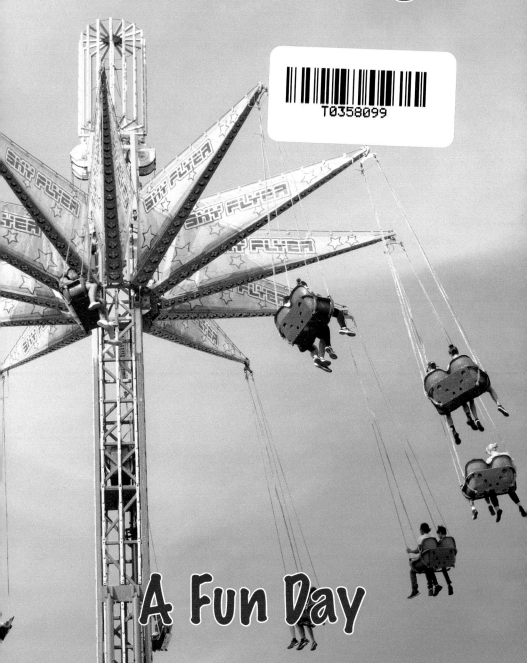

A Fun Day

It is Show Day.

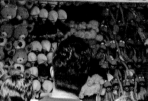

Come and see the cows.

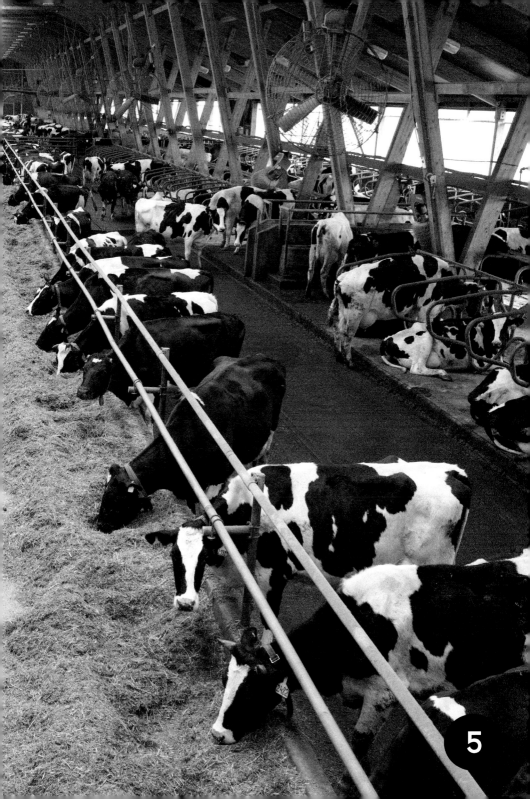

Come and see
the sheep.

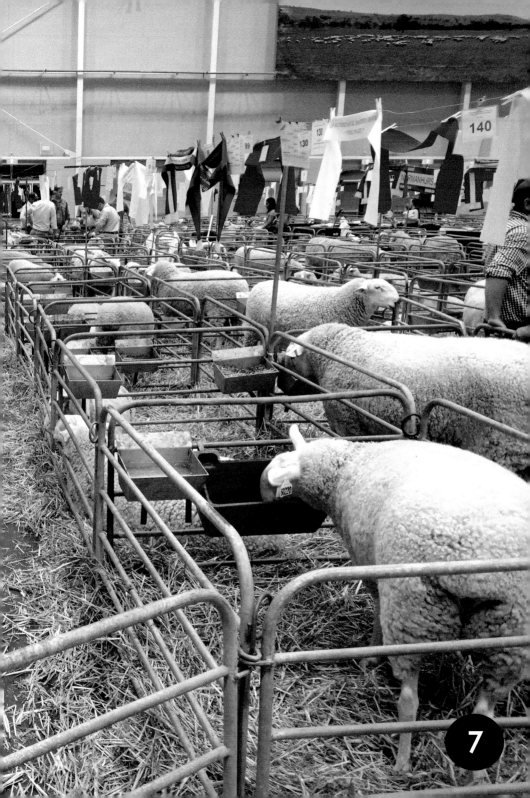

7

Come and see

the chicks.

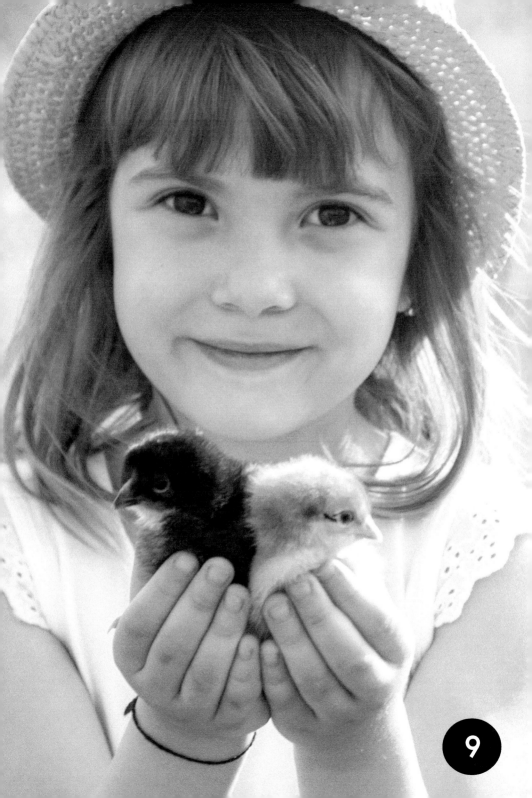

Come and see
the clowns.

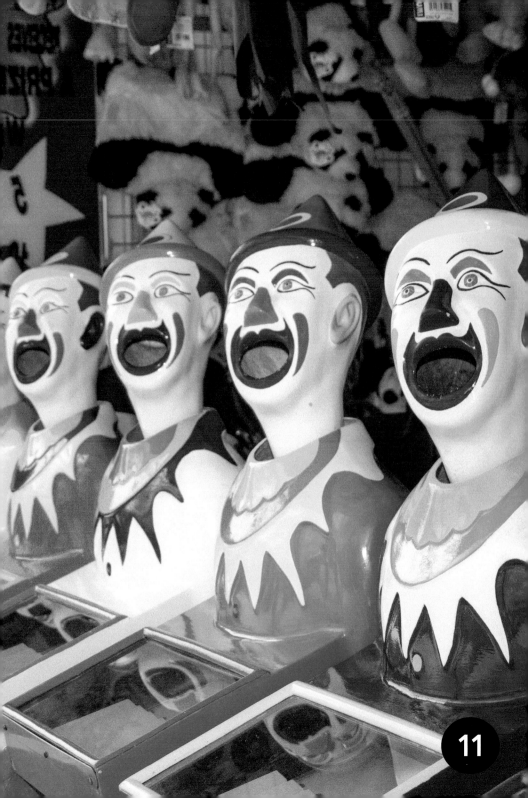

11

Come and see the fairyfloss.

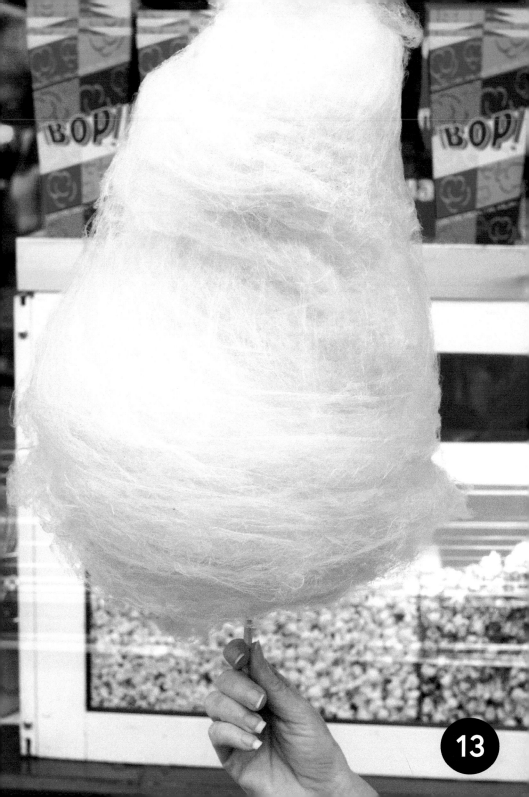

Come and see
the fireworks.

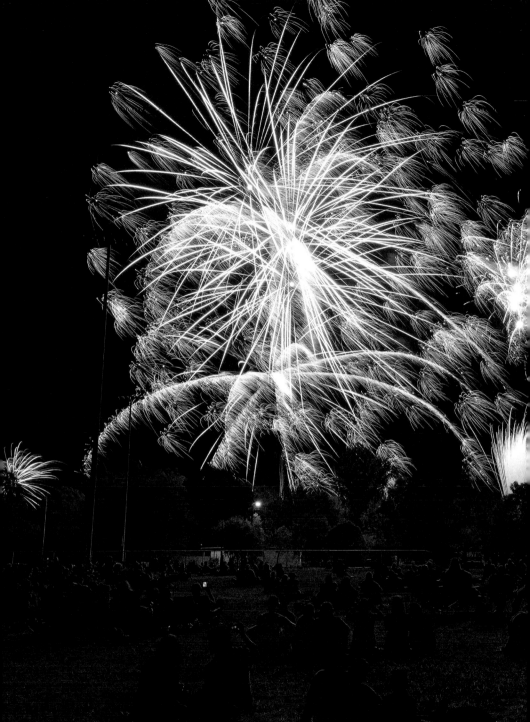

Come and see
my showbag.

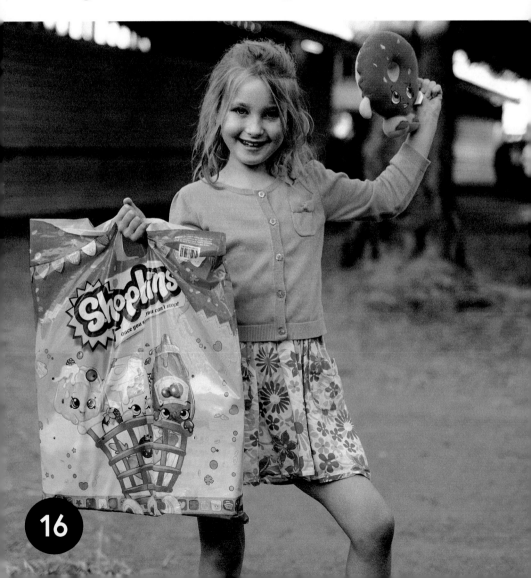